Pebble®
Bilingüe/
Bilingual Plus

Perros de trabajo/Working Dogs

Perros de terapia
Therapy Dogs

por/by Kimberly M. Hutmacher

Editora consultora/Consulting Editor: Gail Saunders-Smith, PhD

Consultora/Consultant: Linda Murray, evaluadora/evaluator
Therapy Dogs International

CAPSTONE PRESS
a capstone imprint

Pebble Plus is published by Capstone Press,
1710 Roe Crest Drive, North Mankato, Minnesota 56003.
www.capstonepub.com

 Books published by Capstone Press are manufactured with paper containing at least 10 percent post-consumer waste.

Library of Congress Cataloging-in-Publication Data
Hutmacher, Kimberly.
 [Therapy dogs. Spanish & English]
 Perros de terapia = Therapy dogs / por/by Kimberly M. Hutmacher.
 p. cm.—(Pebble plus bilingüe/bilingual. Perros de trabajo = Working dogs)
 Includes index.
 Summary: "Simple text and full-color photos illustrate the traits, training, and duties of therapy dogs—in both English and Spanish"—Provided by publisher.
 ISBN 978-1-4296-6902-3 (library binding)
 1. Dogs—Therapeutic use—Juvenile literature. 2. Working dogs—Juvenile literature. I. Title. II. Title: Therapy dogs. III. Series.
 RM931.D63H8818 2012
 636.73—dc22   2011000646

Editorial Credits
Erika Shores, editor; Strictly Spanish, translation services; Bobbie Nuytten, designer; Danielle Ceminsky,
    bilingual book designer; Marcie Spence, media researcher; Laura Manthe, production specialist

Photo Credits
AP Images/Casa Grande Dispatch, Alan Levine, 17; Independence Daily Reporter, Nick Wright, 21
Capstone Studio/Karon Dubke, 19
Getty Images Inc./Chris Jackson, cover, 1
Landov LLC/Boston Globe/Bill Polo, 5
Newscom, 13, 15; Dave Williams/Wichita Eagle, 11; Eliza Gutierrez, 9
Super Stock Inc., 7

Note to Parents and Teachers

The Perros de trabajo/Working Dogs series supports national social studies standards related to people, places, and culture. This book describes and illustrates therapy dogs in both English and Spanish. The images support early readers in understanding the text. The repetition of words and phrases helps early readers learn new words. This book also introduces early readers to subject-specific vocabulary words, which are defined in the Glossary section. Early readers may need assistance to read some words and to use the Table of Contents, Glossary, Internet Sites, and Index sections of the book.

Printed in the United States of America in North Mankato, Minnesota.
032014
008024R

Table of Contents

Tabla de contenidos

A Helping Paw

Did you know that some dogs have jobs? Therapy dogs work in nursing homes, hospitals, schools, and libraries.

Una pata que ayuda

¿Sabías que algunos perros tienen empleos? Los perros de terapia trabajan en hogares para ancianos, hospitales, escuelas y bibliotecas.

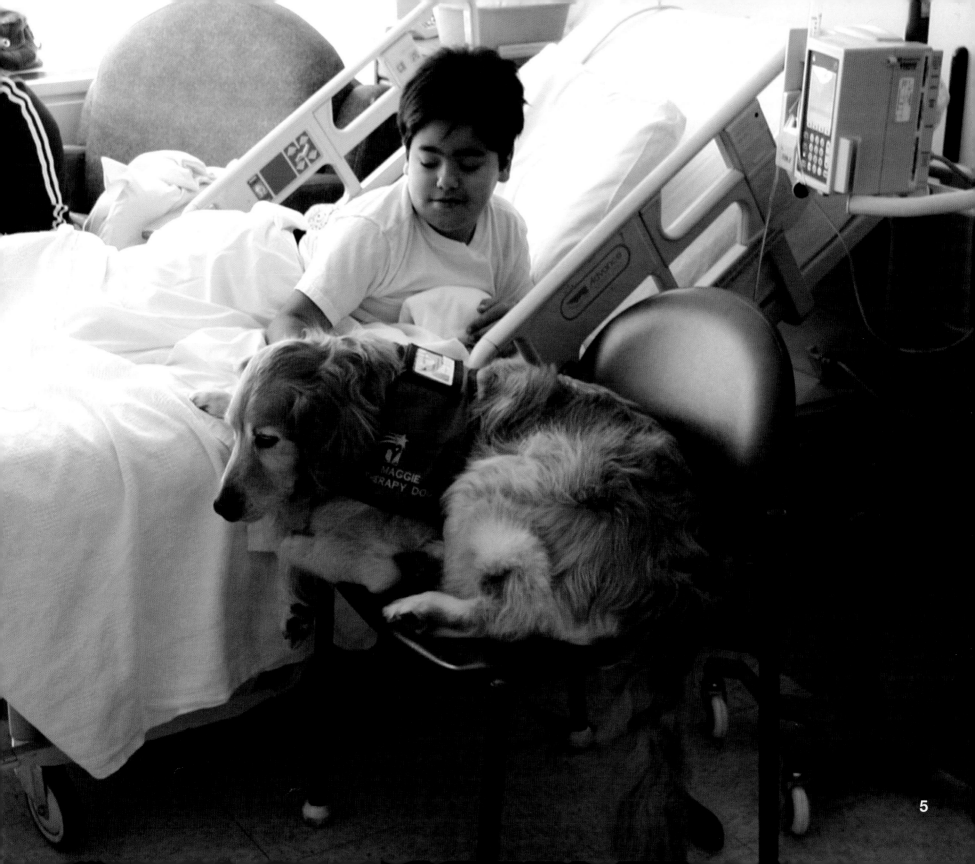

Therapy dogs are friends to people in need. People in hospitals feel better by petting dogs. Elderly people feel less lonely when dogs visit.

Los perros de terapia son amigos de personas con necesidades. Las personas en hospitales se sienten mejor si acarician perros. Las personas ancianas se sienten menos solas cuando los perros las visitan.

Children practice reading to therapy dogs. They think it's more fun to read to dogs than to adults.

Los niños practican leer con perros de terapia. Ellos piensan que es más divertido leerle a un perro que a adultos.

The Right Kind of Dog

All sizes and breeds can be therapy dogs.

The dogs must think and act a certain way.

The way animals act is called their temperament.

El tipo correcto de perro

Todos los tamaños y razas pueden ser perros de terapia. Los perros deben pensar y actuar de cierta manera. La manera en que el animal actúa se llama temperamento.

A therapy dog's temperament
is friendly, calm, and smart.
The dogs are good around
new people, animals, and places.

El temperamento de un perro de
terapia es amigable, tranquilo e
inteligente. Los perros son buenos
alrededor de personas, animales y
lugares nuevos.

Becoming a Therapy Dog

Some owners train therapy dogs. Other dogs go to classes. Dogs learn to always obey commands such as "sit" and "stay."

Cómo entrenar a un perro de terapia

Algunos dueños entrenan perros de terapia. Otros perros van a clases.

Los perros aprenden a siempre obedecer órdenes como "siéntate" o "quédate".

Hospitals have loud machines. During training, dogs hear these machines and other sounds. They learn not to be scared or bark.

Los hospitales tienen máquinas ruidosas. Durante el entrenamiento, los perros escuchan a estas máquinas y otros sonidos. Ellos aprenden a no asustarse y a no ladrar.

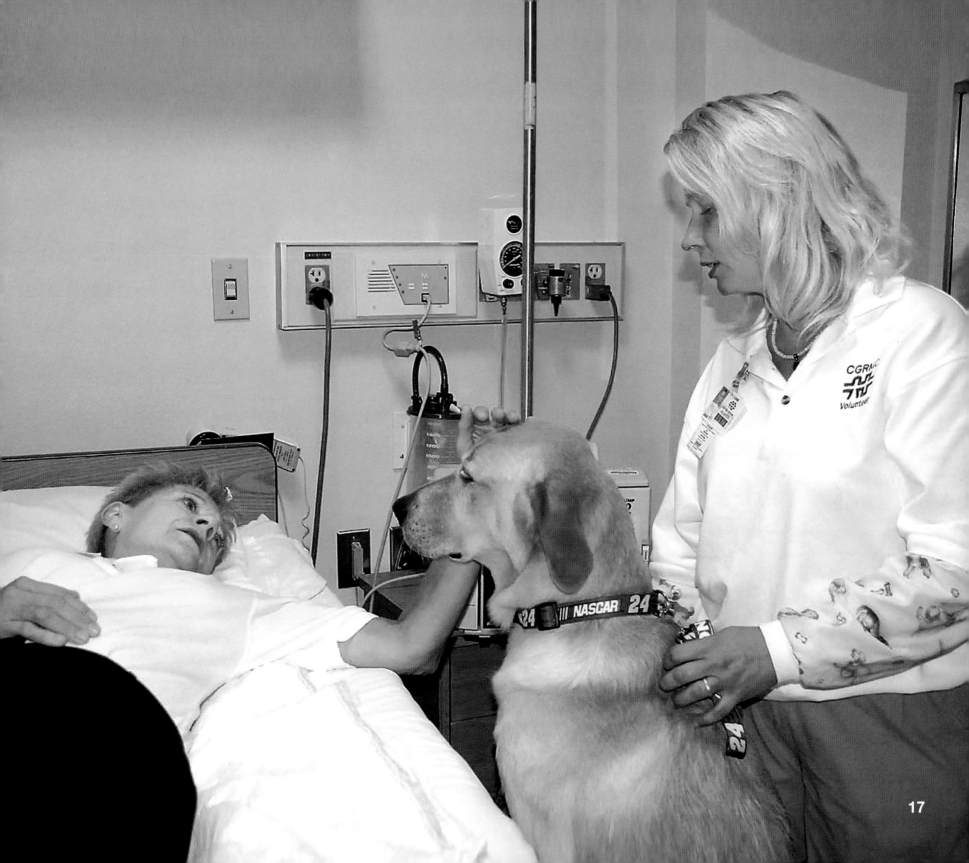

Dogs are tested before becoming therapy dogs. They must walk wearing a loose leash. It proves they follow commands.

Los perros tienen que pasar pruebas antes de ser perros de terapia. Ellos deben caminar usando una correa floja. Esto muestra que ellos pueden seguir órdenes.

Dogs meet new people and dogs during testing. If they stay calm and obey, they pass. Therapy dogs are ready to go to work.

Los perros conocen gente y perros nuevos durante las pruebas. Si permanecen calmos y obedecen, ellos pasan la prueba. Los perros de terapia están listos para comenzar a trabajar.

Glossary

breed—a group of animals that come from common relatives

command—an order to follow a direction

leash—a strap used to hold and control an animal

obey—to follow an order or command

therapy—a treatment for an illness, an injury, or a disability

Internet Sites

FactHound offers a safe, fun way to find Internet sites related to this book. All of the sites on FactHound have been researched by our staff.

Here's all you do:

Visit *www.facthound.com*

Type in this code: 9781429669023

Check out projects, games and lots more at
www.capstonekids.com

Glosario

la correa—una tira usada para sostener y controlar a un animal

obedecer—seguir una orden o comando

las órdenes—comando de seguir una instrucción

la raza—un grupo de animales que provienen de parientes comunes

la terapia—un tratamiento para una enfermedad, una lesión o una discapacidad

Sitios de Internet

FactHound brinda una forma segura y divertida de encontrar sitios de Internet relacionados con este libro. Todos los sitios en FactHound han sido investigados por nuestro personal.

Esto es todo lo que tienes que hacer:

Visita *www.facthound.com*

Ingresa este código: 9781429669023

¡Algo súper divertido! Hay proyectos, juegos y mucho más en www.capstonekids.com

Index

Índice